MOTHER TERESA

a life inspired

About Wyatt North Publishing

Starting out with just one writer, Wyatt North Publishing has expanded to include writers from across the country. Our writers include college professors, religious theologians, and historians.

Wyatt North Publishing provides high quality, perfectly formatted, original books.

Send us an email and we will personally respond within 24 hours! As a boutique publishing company we put our readers first and never respond with canned or automated emails. Send us an email at hello@WyattNorth.com, and you can visit us at www.WyattNorth.com.

Introduction

In 1979, someone asked a small, elderly woman, who was dressed in a simple, perhaps odd-looking, blue and white dress, what an individual could do to promote peace in the world. The woman quickly answered: "Go home and love your family." Coming from such an individual, one might find the answer simple and even a bit naïve. However, this woman was not just any woman; she was Mother Teresa. At the time, she was the leader of a wildly successful international religious community, served as a beacon of hope for the world, and had recently been awarded the Nobel Peace Prize. Obviously, she was not naïve, and she did possess expertise on promoting peace in the world. So what could this seemingly simple response mean?

As we will see in the chapters that follow, Mother Teresa always lived a life in which she was at home and loving her family. This might seem like a strange claim since Mother Teresa constantly traveled the globe, helping the poor and needy around the world. However, this fact should not lead us to discount her claim. Rather, it should encourage us to see in her answer something more than meets the eye—something more complex than what the words might first imply.

Throughout her life, Mother Teresa worked to transform our ideas of home, love, and family. As a figure of the 20th century, she saw the rapid changes taking place in the world and among its people, and she was intuitive enough to know that Catholicism, as well as its missionary work, would need to re-imagine itself in order to meet newly emerging and diverse needs. However, she brought about transformation in a simple and unassuming way. She simply asked individuals to contemplate the meaning of ideas such as home, love, and family and to be open to new conceptions of these terms in the midst of our changing world. In doing so, Mother Teresa introduced a new, modern way of doing missionary work, led an international religious organization, and was beloved by people the world over for the work she did out of love for her family, which would one day grow to include all of humanity.

Chapter One: Mother Teresa's Origins

In August of 1910, in the town of Skopje, in what is today the Republic of Macedonia, a tiny baby named Agnes Gonxha Bojaxhiu came into the world. She was born into an Albanian Catholic family during the calm of the earliest days of the twentieth century, in those brief moments before two World Wars would tear Europe apart, before the threat of communism would consume the West, and before decolonization movements the world over would redraw maps time and time again. This child would never grow to great heights, indeed never reaching more than a mere five feet tall; yet her image, dominated by a smile that engulfed a face of a thousand wrinkles, would be known the world over, and her deeds would distinguish her as one of the 20th century's greatest humanitarians.

It would not be long, only two years in fact, before Agnes's land was consumed by war. Her people would be ostracized and attacked, once for their ethnicity and then again for their religion. With the Ottoman Empire crumbling in the early 1910s, the Balkans, the land immediately west of modern-day Turkey, erupted into the type of violence that can only be fueled by ethnic and religious strife centuries in the making.

Positioned not far from what was once Constantinople, the city that for much of history had been the meeting ground between West and East, the Balkans of the early 20th century was composed of a great diversity of peoples. There were a number of different ethnic groups in the region, including Serbs, Albanians, Bulgarians, Greeks, and Turks. There were a number of religious divisions as well, divisions that at times fell along ethnic lines and at other times cut straight across them. During the early Middle Ages, the region had been dominated by Orthodox Christianity as well as a sizable Jewish population. Later, some in the region, including many Albanians, converted to Catholicism. There was yet another wave of conversions, primarily amongst the Albanian people, as Islam moved into the region and later became the official religion of the Ottoman Empire.

Despite all of this turmoil, Agnes's earliest days were happy and content. She was born to Nikola (father) and Drana (mother) Bojaxhiu. She had two older siblings: a sister, Aga, and a brother, Lazar. The date of her birth is disputed, but Agnes always claimed that her "true" birthday was August 27, the day she was baptized into the Catholic Church. They were a happy family and fairly well-off. Nikola worked a number of odd jobs, and the family attended their local Catholic church. However, as the ethnic and religious strife of the region came to Skopje, Nikola became increasingly involved in city politics.

With the fall of the Ottoman Empire, the power structure that had kept the numerous differences of the region in check disappeared as well. Violence erupted not only between the different ethnic groups of the region but also amongst the different religions. During Agnes's earliest days, the Serbs, a majority of whom practiced the Orthodox faith, were able to step in and fill the political vacuum in the region. The Albanians quickly found themselves living in a land that was not their own, both ethnically and religiously. As a result, an Albanian Independence movement grew quickly in numbers and support, and Nikola became increasingly involved in its activities. This movement resulted in the creation of an Albanian state in 1912. The drawing of such national borders is, of course, always the result of arbitrary and political decisions, and thus a great number of Albanians, including those living in Skopje, found themselves living in lands not contained within these borders. What is more, the Albanian nation that was created was dominated by those of the Muslim religion, leaving Catholic Albanians torn between their nation and their faith. Families such as the Bojaxhius thus found themselves in increasingly complicated and dangerous times. As Albanians, they had, overnight, become foreigners in the Serbian-dominated lands in which they lived, yet the nation that they might have called home did not reflect their religious convictions.

These regional tensions were only heightened and exacerbated with the outbreak of World War One in 1914. The war was instigated by the assassination of Archduke Ferdinand of Austria in Sarajevo, another Balkan city only a day's travel from Skopje. Soon after, the European powers began to move into the area, further fueling the ethnic and religious differences in the region in order to use them for their own global ends.

Little is know for certain about Nikola's actions at this time. As an Albanian, was he working with factions of the independence movement that wanted to extend the national borders to include the city of Skopje as well? Or was he working with other, smaller fringe factions, which aimed to ensure the safety and freedom of the region's Catholic minority to practice its faith alongside the Orthodox Christians and Muslims who dominated regional politics? Perhaps all we may ever know for certain is that Nikola died, quite quickly and unexpectedly, in 1919, when Agnes was only eight or nine years old. There has been much speculation, but no answers, as to the cause of his death. It is widely thought, however, that he was likely poisoned by one of any number of political foes.

What must it have been like for young Agnes, growing up in such tumultuous times? One can only imagine the conversations that would have taken place around the dinner table and that might have formed her earliest memories. These might have included impassioned speeches about devotion to one's religion and people and about the will to stand up for one's identity and beliefs, even in the face of the harshest and most violent adversity. Such ideas must have been staples of Agnes's early life. However, these political teachings absorbed from her father would find new meaning as Drana, Agnes's mother, took charge of the family in the wake of Nikola's death. Drana began turning the family away from the treachery of politics and toward the safety and compassion of the Church.

Chapter Two: Her Father's Death and the Turn Toward Religion

Nikola's death devastated the family. Not only had they lost their father; they had also lost their sole bread-winner. They quickly went from a comfortable middle-class lifestyle to one in which food was scarce and times were hard. Despite their hardships, Drana, Agnes's mother, was unwavering in her faith in God's goodness and compassion. Drana was the family's rock, and Agnes became extremely close with her. Thus, as Drana increasingly turned to the church and its teachings to sustain herself, so too did Agnes and the rest of the family.

One teaching that the family took especially seriously, and quite literally, was Jesus' command to love thy neighbor as thyself. This is most obvious from the way in which their dinners began to change. The tumultuous times in Skopje, and the region at large, had produced disastrous effects not only for the Bojaxhiu family but also for many other ordinary individuals and families. Skopje began to fill up with destitute people—victims of the catastrophic violence in the region who had lost their homes, families, and livelihoods. Drana, in the face of such desperate need, threw open the doors of her house and began to invite the hungry and needy to join her family at their dinner table. Indeed, it seemed that no matter how scarce the family's food reserves became, Drana was always able to add another dinner plate to the table. She refused to let others go hungry if her family was able to eat. As we will see, this was a lesson Agnes would carry with her throughout her life: whatever one had was never so scarce that it could not be divided and shared with another in need. As Drana told the young Agnes, "My child, never eat a single mouthful unless you are sharing it with others."

For a long time, Agnes assumed that the individuals who joined her family at dinner were friends from town or church. However, upon asking her mother once about those who joined them at their table, Drana responded, "Some of them are our relations, but all of them are our people." How different the dinners at the Bojaxhiu household had become! When her father was alive and the family was directly embroiled in the political events of Skopje and the region at large, meals were most likely filled with conversations about political tensions and oppositions outlining "us" versus "them": Serbs versus Albanians; Christians versus Muslims; Catholics versus Orthodox. Now, these lines and concerns began to blur into the background as any hungry person, whether Albanian or Serb, Orthodox or Catholic, was welcome in their home and at their table.

In fact, her commitment to others led Agnes to learn the Serbian-Croatian language, and she began serving as a translator for individuals at the family's church and in other situations. The distinctions that so divided the region continued to disintegrate for her as she began to form deep connections with members of groups other than her own. In short, the family's turn toward religion, initiated by her mother in response to her father's death, was creating a shift in whom Agnes understood to be her "people"—that is, to which individuals she felt connected and of which groups she felt herself to be a part. In place of political, ethnic, and religious divisions, Agnes was beginning to see everyone as members of one community, united through Christ's sacrifice and in God's love.

However, it was not by means of these dinners alone that the family put their Catholic faith into practice. In the summers, they joined their church on a month-long pilgrimage to the shrine of Our Lady of Cernagore, located in what is today Letnica, Kosovo. These pilgrimages took the family into the mountains north of the city and were a happy relief for Agnes. Skopje is located at the base of a valley, with the Vardar River running right through its city center. The climate is fairly warm and humid, and this took a toll on the sickly Agnes, who suffered through both malaria and whooping cough as a child. For Agnes, these pilgrimages were not only spiritually fulfilling but also a healthy retreat to a more temperate and agreeable climate.

There is little doubt that these pilgrimages were a formative time for Agnes's relationship with God. They healed her body and also served her soul, giving her time to reflect and contemplate, which came naturally to the serious, introverted child. These reflections prompted the development of the highly personal connection she felt with God, the depths of which the world would come to know only after her death.

Drana's lessons about God's love and Jesus' commandment to love one's neighbor, whatever their religion and ethnicity might be, would be fundamental to Agnes's future actions and achievements. Indeed, Agnes would take these beliefs and further expand upon them until the whole world would truly become her people. This, however, does not mean that Agnes did not gain anything from her father's more political sensibilities, for the world in which Agnes was growing up in and in which she would become an actor of global consequence was rapidly changing. The political lessons Agnes learned from her father would serve her many times throughout her life as she brought love for God and neighbor to the world's poor and those afflicted by colonialism and the decolonization movements, cold wars, cultural wars, and many other 20th-century affairs.

Chapter Three: Mother Teresa's First Religious Calling

Drana's strength and commitment to the church, as well as the family's yearly visits to a shrine devoted to the Virgin Mother, taught Agnes yet another important lesson. In the Virgin, as well as in her mother, she saw the enormous potential that women of faith had and the impact that they could have on the world. Through these two figures, Agnes learned that she did not need to sit on the sidelines; the power of God flowed through her, and she could have an overwhelmingly positive effect on "her people."

It was on one of her family's summer pilgrimages, in 1922, that Agnes first felt called to a religious life. She was twelve at the time, and it was then that she knew she would devote her life to doing God's work. At the time, she was not exactly sure what this meant, but she put her faith in God and threw herself into church activities.

It was for this reason that she began to learn about the long history of Catholic missionary work, including missions to the land today known as India. She loved hearing stories about the exotic lands and the difficult but fulfilling work of the missionaries. She began to dream of going on such adventures herself. However, in the 1920s, missionary work was done almost exclusively by men. What was a young girl with hopes and dreams like those of Agnes to do?

Luckily, a priest at her church introduced her to an Irish order of nuns known as the Loreto Sisters of Dublin. The order was founded in the 17th century and had, from its inception, been doing pioneering work. Since the 17th century, the nuns had journeyed throughout the world, serving as teachers to the local children of whatever land they found themselves in. They even had schools in India, the land that most excited Agnes's interest and compassion. In 1841, twelve nuns from the Sisters of Loreto had traveled to the Indian city of Calcutta in order to establish a school there. Their success in India grew quickly. By 1842, they had 60 students at their school, called Loreto House, and within three years they had expanded to three boarding schools and three days schools and had established two orphanages as well.

Here was the opportunity for which Agnes had been praying! Here was a group of women who—like Mary, the Virgin mother, as well as her own mother—did not sit back passively; they took an active role in bringing God's word to the world. What is more, they did so in the very land that so ignited Agnes's imagination. Finally, Agnes understood the meaning of the calling that she had first felt at only twelve years of age. In 1928, Agnes decided to join the Loreto Sisters of Dublin and become a nun.

We must not think that this was an easy decision for the young Agnes. Far from it. After much prayer and introspection, she was certain that this was what God had called her to do. However, devoting herself to God and becoming a nun for an Irish order, with the hope of one day teaching in India, would mean leaving her family, her church, and the land in which she had grown up, all of which she loved fiercely. Perhaps even more significantly, it would mean leaving her mother, her rock, with the possibility that she might never see her again. Indeed, Agnes agonized over her decision, as did her mother. However, Drana, who as her daughter's role model understood Agnes's devotion to God so well, was the one who, in the end, insisted that this was what Agnes must do with the rest of her life.

And so, at the tender age of 18, Agnes packed up the few possessions she would need, left everyone and everything she had ever known, and journeyed to a new and foreign land. She did not go to India immediately. Rather, she traveled to Dublin, where the main branch of the Sisters of Loreto was located. It was here that Agnes would spend her postulancy, the time period (lasting anywhere from six months to a year) during which an individual lives with the order she plans to join, takes part in their daily activities, and prays to God to determine whether she has, in fact, correctly understood her calling and has made the right decision in choosing to become a nun.

In addition to praying, Agnes also spent a lot of time learning more about the history of the order and their teaching exploits around the world, and she practiced the English language. This was the primary language of the order and also the language in which she would be expected to teach in India. Agnes, of course, missed her mother and the rest of her family terribly. However, by the end of 1928, she was certain that she had made the right choice in devoting her life to the work of God and was excited to set off on new adventures.

In another way, Agnes's decision to join the Sisters of Loreto and leave her homeland in search of foreign adventures was a pragmatic and fortuitous one. The end of the First World War in November of 1918 had left the Balkans in ruins. What stability had arisen in the region during the 1910s after the fall of the Ottomans, if any, was wiped away by the onslaught of global politics and occupation by European powers. What is more, the League of Nations, an international body founded after World War One and meant to maintain world peace by determining ethnic and territorial disputes, began imposing new and arbitrary political boundaries in the region. Again ethnicities and religions were divided by national borders, and in response, massive deportations and relocations were initiated throughout the region. The war, as well as the later population movements, devastated the region socially and economically.

In short, Agnes confronted a dire situation in her homeland. What possible future was there for her if she remained in Skopje? In many ways, perhaps it was better for her to leave her homeland and make a new start. True, the land to which she would journey, and which she would ultimately call her new home and country, was itself on the verge of monumental and often violent change, but there was also the potential to do God's work there and serve her fellow man. With that intention, Agnes bravely set out into the world.

Chapter Four: Voyage to India

On December 1, 1928, with her postulancy at an end, Agnes boarded a boat with a fellow friend and nun and set off for India. Five weeks later, after a long and arduous voyage at sea, she arrived in Darjeeling, on January 5, 1929. Finally, she was in the land of which she had dreamed for so long. It was here that she would spend her novitiate period, lasting a total of two years. The novitiate period is a time between a future nun's postulancy and her taking of vows. In this time period, both the future nun and her order have agreed that she has been called to a life of service and devotion to God. The novitiate is thus the period during which a woman learns all that will be expected of her once she takes her vows and becomes a nun. For Agnes, this meant her continued study of English in preparation for her teaching duties. She also began to study both the Bengali and Hindi languages so that, when the time came, she would be better able to serve the people around her.

The land that had once been a mere figment of her wildest dreams quickly became a reality for the young Agnes. In some ways she found herself in a land rather similar to the homeland she had left behind, but in other ways the country and its culture were markedly different. Agnes had much to learn.

Like the Balkans, India is a land afflicted by ancient ethnic and religious differences that have erupted into violence at numerous times throughout the centuries. It is home to many different groups of people as well as many different religions. The majority of Indians practice Hinduism; however, beginning in the 12th century, a sizable Muslim minority began to develop. Since the 15th century, there has been a substantial number of Sikhs, practitioners of a monotheistic religion that originated in the northwestern region of India. India is also home to many Christians. Missionary work in India had been occurring for centuries before groups such as the Sisters of Loreto arrived to the land in the 19th century. In fact, the first Catholic missionaries were from Portugal and came as early as the 1500s, at the beginning of European voyage and expansion around the globe.

Missionary presence in India, including the schools started and maintained by the Sisters of Loreto, did increase considerably in the 1800s, thanks in large part to British colonial rule. For centuries, India had been the spice capital of the world, and the economic and political ties between India and Europe—and Britain in particular—were long and deep. The East India Company, an English trade organization, was first formed in 1600 and took exclusive trading rights over all business involving Indian goods and resources. Due to the company's financial success in the region, the land became an official colony of the British Empire in 1612. By the 1800s, the British Empire was at its height; it was a tightly-knit, well-oiled machine that spanned the globe. This impressive organization made possible the type of social work that missionaries carried out.

However, by the early 1900s, Britain's empire was crumbling. Its sway over its lands was rapidly dwindling, due in large part to toll that the First World War had taken on England. Confronted by real and immediate dangers at home, English was unable to continue to support and control its far-flung colonies around the globe. By the end of the 1920s, India was a land on the verge of massive change and upheaval. In 1930, just a year after Agnes's arrival in India, a disobedience movement advocating nonviolent methods such as hunger strikes arose, led by the famed Mahatma Gandhi. This movement called for an end to British colonial rule and the beginning of Indian self-governance. Yet again, Agnes found herself in a land where people were divided and political power and borders were unstable and fraught.

In addition to this political unrest, Agnes also confronted a social system unlike anything she had experience in her homeland or in her short time in Dublin. The caste system in India has a long and complicated history, made even more complex by the British government's exploitation of the system in order to maintain peace in the country during colonial times. What can be said for certain is that, by the time Agnes arrived in India, the caste system was a deep-seated and powerful social organization that had an impact on the minds and daily realities of the Indian people. According to the caste system, people were divided into groups, including Brahmins, Kshatriyas, Vaishyas, and Shudras. Each group served a different role in society. Brahmins were known as the priestly caste, Kshatriayas were the warriors, Vaishyas were merchants and landowners, and Shudras were the servant class. Group membership was inherited according to birth, and divisions between the groups, even those involving such basic social interactions as interactions in a shop or a nod on the street, were strictly maintained. Each group also possessed differing amounts of social, political, and economic capital, and as a result, they were organized hierarchically, with some groups having much more power than others.

One group in particular, the Dalits, was excluded from this hierarchy completely. Also known as "untouchables," members of this group were thought to have no role and were essentially excluded from taking part in society in any way. They did not—indeed, due to the rigidity of the divisions imposed by the caste system, could not—have direct interactions with members of any of the castes; and if they were even able to find work, they only did the most menial of labor. As a result, they were poor and downtrodden and had little ability or support within Indian society to improve their situation. This also meant that, as tensions rose in India with the growth of the disobedience movement and waning of British control, this group was disproportionately affected by the negative impact that these tensions had on the Indian population. Disease and hunger were rampant, and because of the social stigma barring interaction between these people and members of other castes, there was little in the way of medical care or social services. In almost all ways, these people had been forgotten, left to suffer and die alone.

In time, these very people, the untouchables of India, would become Agnes's people. That, however, was still years in the future, after Agnes had already lived what many would find to be a full and successful life as a nun and teacher.

On May 24, 1931, Agnes took yet another monumental step in this direction, undertaking her First Profession of Vows and becoming a full member of the Sisters of Loreto. It was at this time that she took the name by which the world would come to remember her by: Teresa. She chose the name in honor of Saint Thérèse of Lisieux. Saint Thérèse, known by many as "The Little Flower," was a French Carmelite nun who died tragically of tuberculosis in 1897 at the young age of 24. Although she had spent much of her short life secluded from the world in a convent, her writings about her deep and personal relationship with God have become known the world over. She was also famous for her devotion to, and prays for priests, especially those conducting missionary work. Upon her canonization, in 1925, she was deemed the patron saint of missionaries.

There is little doubt why Agnes chose the namesake she did. Like Saint Thérèse, she too had participated in a deep and spiritual relationship with God from a young age; and like Saint Thérèse, she was also captivated by the work being done by missionaries. However, unlike her namesake, Agnes would not be content to remain in her convent. Instead, she would go out into the world to meet with, and advocate for, the poor and needy, all the while radically reshaping the way in which missionary work was done.

Chapter Five: Mother Teresa's Teaching Years

Upon becoming a nun, Agnes, now known as Sister Teresa, moved to Calcutta to begin her teaching career. By this time, the Sisters of Loreto had become well-established in Calcutta, known for their superior ability to teach local children English, a highly necessary skill if one were to be successful in Indian society. By the 1930s, the order had established a compound of sorts in Calcutta—a large set of walls that separated their many schools from the city at large. They had a total of 500 students, with a majority coming from wealthy families who were able to pay the tuition necessary to fund and maintain the schools. The nuns left the shelter of the compound walls rarely, if ever. This meant that, given the socioeconomic status of most of their students, they were often unaware of many of the hardships taking place amongst the lowest and most destitute of India's population.

Sister Teresa's situation was a bit different. She began teaching geography and history at Saint Mary's, a school housed within the compound. Unlike many of the other schools, however, Saint Mary's catered to an economically and socially mixed group of students from a variety of backgrounds. What is more, many of the teachers alongside whom she worked were not missionaries who had come to India but, rather, Christian women from India. Many of them had been educated by the Sisters of Loreto and later become nuns themselves. These women did not wear the traditional nun's habit, as Sister Teresa and the other missionary teachers did at the time, but rather wore saris, or traditional Indian dresses.

In this way, Sister Teresa became aware of aspects of Indian society that were unknown to many of her fellow nuns. Her students and fellow teachers offered her intimate accounts documenting the issues faced by many of the lower classes due to the rigid social system in place in India, issues that were only exacerbated by the politics of the time. It was in this way that Sister Teresa was first introduced to the plight of people living right outside the walls of the compound that she called home. The poor and untouchables of Calcutta who were her neighbors now.

She became even more starkly aware of the urgency of their situation when, in 1935, she was given a special exemption to teach at the school of Saint Teresa. The school was located beyond the walls of her order's compound, and this meant that Sister Teresa had to go on daily walks through the city of Calcutta as she commuted to and from the school. It was during the course of these walks that she encountered firsthand what her students and fellow teachers at Saint Mary's could only describe to her. The people's plight was worse than anything she could have imagined, even though she had heard many stories. She encountered poor and unfortunate people everywhere, living alone and starving in dirty, makeshift slums. Many had simply been left to die in the streets, often for no other reason than their lack of social status.

One cannot help but wonder whether, in addition to provoking her love and compassion for the poorest of India, this experience might not also have left Sister Teresa feeling a bit frustrated. She had left everyone and everything she had known and loved behind in order to go off into the world and serve God's people, and certainly, as a Sister of Loreto and a teacher at Saint Mary's, she was doing precisely that. And yet, a mere 10 feet from her classroom, on the other side of a dividing wall, people—her neighbors—were dying in the streets. She could not have helped but notice that within the walls of her compound, by and large, were found those of higher social and economic standing in India while those outside of its walls were the people most negatively affected by such social divisions—those made "untouchable" by the caste system. Sister Teresa had already seen the unnecessary and overwhelmingly negative effects that these types of arbitrary social divisions had caused in her homeland. Indeed, her short life had been filled with the kind of violence to which these types of divisions so often give way. However, thanks to the lessons she had learned from her mother and the family dinners they used to have back in Skopje, Sister Teresa would not be persuaded by, or content with, such divisions. She devoutly knew that all people were her people; all people were one in God. There was surely some way in which she could serve those who most needed her. However, in 1935, such thoughts would only have been in their infancy for Sister Teresa. It would be many years yet before she was able to put them fully into action.

Until that time, Sister Teresa would continue to teach within the compound at Saint Mary's. On May 24, 1937, she took her Final Profession of Vows, fully committing herself to the life of poverty, chastity, and obedience expected of a nun of the Sisters of Loreto. It was at this time that she took on the title of "Mother," giving her the name we all hold so dearly today: Mother Teresa. She was a hard and diligent teacher. She expected much of her students but also showed them endless love. Over the years, she affected many devoted young girls who would later, as women, become her followers.

In 1944, 15 years after she first began to teach in India, Mother Teresa became the principal of Saint Mary's. She was 34 years old, and in many ways she had already achieved everything for which she had hoped and prayed as a little girl while on summer pilgrimages with her family in the mountains north of Skopje. She had become a Sister of Loreto, she had moved to India as a Catholic missionary, and she served the people by teaching their children. Despite all of her success, she would not remain content for long. She could not forget the plight of those people who lived beyond the walls of the compound; they may have been forgotten by the rest of the world, but Mother Teresa would remember them, and she would act.

Chapter Six: Mother Teresa's Second Religious Calling

In 1943, a horrific famine swept across the region. Its causes were numerous. There had been crop failures several years in a row as well as a terrible and destructive cyclone. In addition, the region's resources had been increasingly depleted by the onslaught of World War Two. At home, India was also afflicted by crippling government corruption. In 1935, Britain had passed the Government of India Act. While India remained a British colony, the act granted it a large amount of autonomy. Unfortunately, the young government was not yet stable enough to address such a crisis successfully, and a number of inept policy failures stopped food reserves from reaching the people. Millions perished.

As the principal of her school, Mother Teresa was responsible for her students and her teachers alike. On several occasions during these difficult times, she had to leave the confines of the compound walls in order to search for food. This was an eye-opening experience for her. If her school was suffering from the famine, this suffering was incomparable to that of the city's poor and untouchables who lived beyond the walls of her compound.

The lack of resources, as well as government wrongdoing, increased tensions amongst the different peoples of India.

Most notably, violence began breaking out between the land's Hindu and Muslim populations. Tensions were especially high in Calcutta, a city of millions, the population of which was split between Muslims and Hindus. On August 16, 1946, tensions boiled over in Calcutta. Known today as the "Great Calcutta Killings," riots between Muslims and Hindus erupted throughout the city. Three days later, 4,000 people had been killed, and over 100,000 people had been left homeless.

Mother Teresa just happened to choose August 16, of all days, to go out into the city in search of food for her school. What she saw shocked her. There were people killing each other in the streets while amongst the bodies lay the poor and starving. Calcutta was a city coming apart at the seams. Although teaching children at Saint Mary's was a noble task, surely there was something she could do to address the pain and suffering that surrounded her school. There must be something more she could do for India; there must be something more she could do for her neighbors—for her people.

On September 10, 1946, less than a month after this horrific event, Mother Teresa and the rest of her order left Calcutta by train for their annual retreat in the Himalayan foothills. While they were on this train ride, Christ came to Mother Teresa and spoke to her. He told her that he no longer wanted her to teach; he wanted her to leave the confines of her school to go into the slums and work with the poorest and sickest of India. Later, Mother Teresa would call this day her "Day of Inspiration," the day that God called her for a second time.

Although today this idea might seem commonplace—the idea, that is, to live and work with the people who are the most in need—we ought not overlook how unprecedented Mother Teresa's plan was at the time. As we will remember, missionary work in India, including the work done by the Sisters of Loreto, was made possible in large part by the colonial structures put in place by the British government. Inevitably then, these missions came to reflect the structures that supported them. For example, the colonial system benefited from the maintenance of the caste system because it offered the British government a way to order and control the population. This meant that the British government did not actively address the plight of the untouchables of India, those individuals excluded from the caste system entirely and barred from basic contact with the rest of society.

Similarly, missionaries in India had done much to help the people of India. However, they too did not directly serve the poorest and most needy of India. Instead, as the Sisters of Loreto did, they served India's middle classes. This is not to say that the middle classes of India did not desire or benefit from the word of God; they certainly did. Unfortunately, the social system in place at the time made it such that, by serving those groups, missionaries ended up not serving—or, in the case of the Sisters of Loreto, literally building walls to separate themselves from—the most needy in Indian society. The missionary system that had arisen during the colonial period certainly served some of the people of India, but it did not address the plight of the poor who lived in the slums at the outskirts of society.

Mother Teresa's calling challenged this way of doing missionary work. Indeed, in a world that was quickly changing as postcolonial movements around the globe gained ground in the wake of World War Two and redrew borders, she would offer a radically new way of doing missionary work. In short, she would introduce a modern way of bringing God's word to the people of the world, and in doing so she would propel Catholic missionary work into the 20th century.

Despite God's command, however, accomplishing this feat was no simple task. As a Sister of Loreto, Mother Teresa had taken a vow of obedience to the order. She could not simply pick up her belongings and leave them. Instead, she would have to get special permission from the Vatican to grant her leave from her duties with the Sisters. Thus, Mother Teresa launched a campaign, writing letters to the pope and lobbying her local archbishop; she begged them to allow her to fulfill God's plan for her.

In January of 1948, a year and a half after Christ had come to her, she received approval from His Grace Ferdinand Périer, archbishop of Calcutta, to pursue her new calling. He gave her a year to prove that her plan for a new, modern way of doing missionary work could be successful. He asked her to keep a diary, documenting not only her successes and failures in the community but also her own personal struggles and achievements. Mother Teresa would go on to keep a diary for much of the rest of her life, and its contents, including her documentation of her deep and sometimes complicated relationship with God, would be revealed to the world only after her death.

In August of 1948, her life as a teacher already fulfilled, 38-year-old Mother Teresa left the Loreto convent that she had called home for the last 20 years. Yet again, she was leaving behind everything and everyone she knew and setting off into the world in order to do God's work. She did not, however, enter the slums and immediately begin working with the people. Instead, she left Calcutta and went to stay with a different order of nuns in India, known as the Medical Mission Sisters. She thereby learned the basic nursing skills that were so desperately needed, yet so lacking, amongst the poor and untouchable classes. After six months, she went back to Calcutta and entered the slums.

Chapter Seven: The Origins of the Sisters of Charity

After spending several months training with the Medical Mission Sisters, Mother Teresa returned to the city of Calcutta in December of 1948. But what exactly was she to do for the poor now that she had finally received this opportunity? She would have to be innovative and creative because there was no model for her to follow. The people whom she wanted to help were the very people forgotten by the established colonial systems, whether those systems be governmental or religious.

The first change that she made was to live with the people whom she intended to serve. She did not construct a wall around herself or divide herself from the people she so desperately wanted to serve, as had been the case with the compound of schools operated by the Sisters of Loreto; rather, she moved into the slums with the people. She ate, slept, and passed her days with them. For Mother Teresa, there would never again be a division, physical or otherwise, between her and other people—between her and her neighbors. In this way, she was putting into action the lesson she had learned so long ago around her family's dinner table back in Skopje: just as her mother had invited anyone and everyone who was hungry into their house, so too did Mother Teresa make her home with those most in need. As her mother had taught her, they may not be her relations, but they were "her people."

In order to demonstrate her connection to the poor of India, Mother Teresa even went so far as to change the way she dressed. She decided that she would no longer wear the traditional black and white habit donned by the Sisters of Loreto; instead, she chose to dress in the simple blue and white sari for which she would later become famous. In fact, her dress was similar to the Indian women with whom she had worked at Saint Mary's for so many years. Moreover, its simplicity ensured that she met the poor as their equal, down to the very fabric she wore.

But what would she do besides live as an equal with these people? Obviously, she had a little medical training, thanks to the time she had spent with the Medical Mission Sisters; however, she was no expert in this area. She was, though, an expert in teaching, so she began to teach the children of the slums. She could not simply open up a school since she had no capital. Instead, she began by writing in the dirt with a stick and teaching the children out in the open air. As time went on, she was able to find her own living quarters in the area. She also found a hut, which she could rent at the extremely low rate of five rupees per month, and this served as her first schoolhouse.

In March of 1949, she received a special visitor. Subhasini Das was a former pupil of Mother Teresa's from Saint Mary's, and she had heard of the important work that Mother Teresa had been doing for the poor. She had come to join Mother Teresa and help her with her labors. Subhasini became Mother Teresa's first helper and remained her devoted aid throughout her lifetime. Subhasini was quickly followed by 10 other women. Many were former students like Subhasini, and several others had been teachers alongside Mother Teresa at Saint Mary's. All had been inspired by her—by her commitment to God and her drive to connect with and help the poor of India.

This was an extremely significant moment for Mother Teresa. Most importantly, she was no longer a single individual acting upon Jesus' calling; now she was the leader of a small but growing religious community that was the embodiment of this calling. Her growing community was also a tangible mark of her success. Practically speaking, this was crucial if she was to fulfill the archbishop's command to prove herself within a year. This success ensured that she and her vision would retain the support of the Church.

1949 was a significant year for Mother Teresa in another way as well, for it was in this year that she applied for and received her Indian citizenship. In doing so, she had completely re-envisioned who she saw as her "people," thanks in large part to the lessons of her mother. It had not been enough to live with, dress like, and work amongst the poor; now she shared her national allegiance with them as well. How far she had come from her early beginnings and her father's involvement in the fight for the rights of Catholic Albanians. She had crossed oceans and traveled to new lands, and now she found herself united not only with people of a different ethnicity than her own but also many people who did not even share her religion. But such were no longer Mother Teresa's concerns, for now, as a servant of God, she was doing Jesus' will by serving those most in need, no matter their earthly allegiances. She knew that, in God's eyes, they were all His children and, therefore, they were all her neighbors; she was merely doing His will by serving them.

This is not to say that the political lessons she had learned from her father were not useful to her at this time. Indeed, far from it. India had gained its independence from Britain on August 15, 1947. At the same time that the country was shedding the trappings of colonial rule and re-imagining itself as the world's most populous democracy, so too was Mother Teresa re-imagining missionary work in a world after colonialism. The political timeliness of her actions should not be overlooked. By the late 1940s, India was ripe for change, both politically and socially, and Mother Teresa was wise enough to make the most of this moment. By transforming the way in which missionary work was performed, she was ensuring that the Catholic Church would be able to adapt its message to a changing world. This type of transformation could only be achieved by an extremely intelligent and politically aware mind.

On October 7, 1950, Mother Teresa officially received the acknowledgment that she had sought upon leaving the walls of the Sisters of Loreto. On this day, Pope Pius XII bestowed canonical recognition on her growing religious community. Now her group of Catholic women, primarily Indian women who had first met her as teachers and students during her days at Saint Mary's, became known as the congregation of the "Missionaries of Charity" in the Archdiocese of Calcutta. Their official mission was to "serve the suffering Christ, whom they saw in the poorest of the poor."

Chapter Eight: The Early Days of the Sisters of Charity

Mother Teresa and the newly recognized Sisters of Charity did not take their mission lightly. She demanded that they lead a very regimented day. They awoke early in the morning, took a short lunch, and went to bed long after dark. Much of their day was devoted to direct interaction with the poor, teaching and caring for them. A portion of every day was also set aside for prayer and contemplation. If the sisters served Christ by serving the poor, then they needed to cultivate and develop their relationship with God in order to ground their work in His love.

Their numbers quickly grew, and as they did, so too did the number of people they were able to serve. Using her political acumen, Mother Teresa began to take advantage of a law recently passed by the new government. This law stated that, for every 100 children, the government was required to build and maintain a school building. The more women who joined her ranks, the more teachers she was able to train; and the more teachers she had, the more children her sisters were able to serve. In this way, Mother Teresa was able to have several school buildings built without spending any of her own money.

Thanks to the good work her sisters were doing, she began to come to the attention of Indian officials. Independence had not been easy for the young nation. The country continued to be rocked by the same ethnic and religious violence that had so impacted Mother Teresa during her time with the Sisters of Loreto. In fact, just a month after gaining its independence from Great Britain, these tensions literally tore the country apart as the land was partitioned into India and Pakistan. This was followed by widespread violence and bloodshed, resulting in the deaths of hundreds of thousands of people. India was further shaken by the assassination of Mahatma Gandhi in 1948, followed by a war with Pakistan over the disputed territory of Kashmir. In short, the young government was so consumed by political troubles that it had little time or energy to focus on its own citizens, especially the poorest and most destitute. Mother Teresa and the Sisters of Charity filled this void, and the government was thankful for and supportive of all of the important work they were doing.

For this reason, several Indian officials came to Mother Teresa's aide in her first attempts to branch out from education. They helped her to locate and fund the conversion of a deserted Hindu temple into her first home for the dying. Ever since her first trip beyond the walls of the Sisters' of

Loreto compound, Mother Teresa had been distraught by the numbers of individuals she had encountered who were, quite literally, left to die alone in the streets. Most, if not all, of these individuals were member of the untouchable class, and it was therefore taboo for any individual of a different caste to interact with them. As a result, those individuals who were best able to help and support these individuals—doctors, nurses, social workers and so on—did not do so and, at least according to social convention, were unable to do so. Mother Teresa, as well as the Indian officials who supported her, hoped that her home for the dying would fill this void and offer solace to these poor souls in their hour of need. The home opened on August 22, 1952, and was called Kalighat or Nirmal Hriday, which in English means "Place of the Immaculate Heart."

She and the Sisters of Charity branched out yet again in 1955. By this time they had developed a firmly established network of schools for the children who lived in the slums of Calcutta. However, many of these same children were living on the streets, and a great number of them had been orphaned, whether because of rampant disease and lack of healthcare in these areas or because of the pervasive violence that continued to afflict the country. Mother Teresa realized that it was not enough simply to teach these children; she and her sisters needed to give them a home. For this reason, the Sisters of Charity opened up their first orphanage, which they called Nirmala Shishu Bhavan, or the Children's Home of the Immaculate Heart. This home was only the first of many, and by 1958 the sisters had facilities for 90 children.

Around this same time, Mother Teresa also realized that not only was the caste system barring many of Calcutta's poorest from obtaining health services but so too was their inability, whether because of illness or due to lack of resources, to travel to such services. She therefore organized her first mobile clinic in 1956. The vehicle was outfitted with all of the needs of a medical clinic and traveled throughout Calcutta's slums, seeking out individuals in need of care.

These early homes and services were essential for the later development of the Sisters of Charity, for through them, Mother Teresa was able to establish her general approach to caring for those in need and her new, modern approach to missionary work. In all of her endeavors, she offered individuals both support for their most pressing material needs—whether access to education or healthcare or a safe and comforting place to live and die—and spiritual rejuvenation and salvation. Through Mother Teresa's work, many of India's poor were introduced to Jesus Christ for the first time. In short, Mother Teresa cared for and supported individuals in their needs for this life as well as the next.

Mother Teresa's approach was also influenced by the dinners that her mother used to host back in Skopje. Just as her mother had always found a way to share their meager food rations with any and all who joined their family at the dinner table, so too did Mother Teresa ensure that she and the Sisters of Charity shared all of their wealth and solace with as many people as possible. This meant that her orphanages, clinics, and homes often offered only modest accommodations. However, as her mother had taught her so many years before, there was never so little that it could not be divided and shared with others. Mother Teresa took this lesson to heart and was always concerned with the number of individuals she was able to support.

This was an essential part of the way in which Mother Teresa was beginning to re-imagine Catholic missionary work in the changing world of the late 1940s and 1950s. In the wake of postcolonial movements around the globe, as with the events taking place in India, vast numbers of poor individuals who had been excluded and oppressed by the recently ousted colonial system were now emerging from the hidden margins of society. The numbers of people in need of help skyrocketed. Mother Teresa realized that missionary work would have to vastly re-conceptualize the sheer numbers of people whom these projects would be able to serve in the coming years, and she enacted the lessons of her mother in order to do so.

Around this time, Mother Teresa's work began to come to the attention of the Indian press, and several articles were written about her good deeds. These articles earned her many devoted admirers, and those with the means began to donate to the Sisters of Charity. Mother Teresa immediately used these increased funds to open more homes and clinics. Her impact on the poor of India was beginning to increase rapidly.

According to canon law, a new order such as the Missionaries of Charity could not open up a second mission until 10 years after its original founding. This rule, of course, was meant to ensure the success of the original mission, barring it from stretching itself and its resources too thin, too soon. Mother Teresa, made impatient by this rule given her immense success, began making plans to expand to other Indian cities, and she opened several missions a few months before the 10-

year deadline. In 1963, with the opening of the Missionary Brothers of Charity, the Missionaries of Charity officially expanded to include men as well.

In 1960, Mother Teresa embarked upon yet another new and previously unthinkable project. Today many of us may think of leprosy as a thing of the past, even perhaps of the Biblical past. However, this was not the case in India during the middle of the twentieth century. In fact, on the outskirts of many cities, including Calcutta, makeshift colonies of lepers had sprung up, and as many as 30,000 individuals afflicted with the disease lived in India alone. These colonies were places of disease and suffering, avoided by most out of fear of contamination. Placing her trust in God, however, Mother Teresa went into these colonies without fear for herself, intent upon easing the suffering of those living there. She even opened up a home for lepers, known as Shanti Nagar or Place of Peace.

In addition to the ways in which Mother Teresa was transforming missionary work, there are two other important conclusions to be drawn from these early, developmental days of the Missionaries of Charity. The first is Mother Teresa's organizational and political skill and dexterity. In only a few years and with little money, she was able to create a vast network of homes and clinics that served the diverse needs of India's poorest communities. Furthermore, she did so in such a way that she was able to capitalize upon the domestic political void in India, which was a consequence of its government's international concerns and laws. The second lesson is Mother Teresa's ever-expanding understanding of who composed "her people" and of who she would consider to be her neighbors. With the expansion not simply into the slums of India but also into the country's leper colonies, Mother Teresa was showing the world that all people— whether tabooed, diseased, or both—no matter what society thought of them, were her people. She truly understood the claim that all people are God's children and, thus, all people were her neighbors. With this in mind, she organized the Missionaries of Charity so that they fully embodied and acted upon this principle.

Chapter Nine: Mother Teresa's First Trip Abroad

Mother Teresa's success, as well as the new approach to missionary work that she was developing, had caught the eye not only of the Indian press but also of people outside the borders of India. Catholics around the globe increasingly began to talk about the little woman in India, in the simple blue and white sari, who was doing so much good for the poor and destitute. Many people, especially many Catholic women, began looking upon her as a role model. It was for this reason that Mother Teresa was invited to visit the United States in 1960 and speak at the annual meeting of the National Council for Catholic Women in Las Vegas, Nevada.

This would be the first time in 30 years that Mother Teresa would step foot outside the borders of her adopted homeland of India. She traveled to Las Vegas and gave her speech. Mother Teresa spoke frankly and simply to her audience, in what would become known as her characteristic style. She spoke of her devotion to God. She spoke about her conviction that one served Jesus when one served the poorest of the poor. Speaking of her compassion for God's people, she challenged her audience to re-imagine who those people were and whom they might consider to be their neighbors. Just as her mother had taught her that God did not see ethnic divisions such as Albanian or Serbian, Mother Teresa now taught her audience that God did not see divisions such as rich or poor, Western or Eastern, Catholic or Hindu. All of humanity was God's people, and thus a commitment to God meant a commitment to help the poorest and most destitute of humanity, whoever and wherever they might be. She spoke straight from the heart and without notes. Although many had known of her before this time, this speech certainly thrust her into the spotlight for Catholics in America.

From Nevada, she continued her tour of the United States, stopping in both Illinois and New York. Her time in New York left a lasting impression on her as she found the city to be in need of exactly the type of work that she and the Missionaries of Charity did. A little more than 10 years later, she would have the opportunity to act upon this belief.

She decided to take this opportunity to travel to Europe as well before returning to India. She went to London, Germany, and Switzerland and was met by throngs of supporters at every stop. She also stopped in Rome, where her brother had taken up residence after fleeing their war-torn and devastated homeland in the Balkans. Mother Teresa had not see Lazar in over 30 years, and their lives had taken very different paths. Lazar had joined the Albanian army as a young man. During

World War Two, Albania was occupied by Italy, and Lazar had joined the Italian army and become a fervent support of its fascist regime. Despite their differences, they were overjoyed to see one another. They even attempted to devise a plan to have Mother Teresa visit her mother and sister, who had remained in the Balkans and were living in Albania. Unfortunately, after World War Two, Albania had become a ruthless communist regime, tightly controlled by its government. There was no way for Drana and Aga to leave Albania and no way for Mother Teresa, quickly becoming a Western celebrity and thus a potential enemy of the Albanian state, to enter the country. Sadly, this is as close as Mother Teresa would ever come to seeing her mother again.

While in Rome, she was granted an audience with the pope at the time, John XXIII. What a monumental moment this must have been for Mother Teresa. She had been a devoted Catholic for such a long time and had committed her life to serving Jesus, and the opportunity to meet the leader of her religion must have been overwhelming, to say the least. Nevertheless, always keenly aware of the opportunities presented to her, she used the occasion to ask the pope to consider granting her the decree that would allow the Missionaries of Charity to expand internationally. Here we find yet more evidence of

Mother Teresa's exceptional political sensibility, inherited from her father, and a prime example of the way she used this gift to do the will of God and serve her people—that is, the people of the world.

By 1960, the year of this tour, Mother Teresa was 50 years old, and in many ways she had already had the successes of two lifetimes. For almost 20 years, she had been a beloved teacher and principal. Then she had become the founder of an extremely successful new religious order in India that was reshaping Catholic missionary work. For many people, this would have been more than enough; they would have been satisfied with their life's work. Not so for Mother Teresa. She used this trip as the opportunity to open up yet another chapter of her life and find another means by which she might serve the living Christ and cater to the poorest of the poor.

However, it was not only the pope's decree that she and her sisters would need if they wanted to begin working internationally. They would also need money, for such an endeavor would be incredibly expensive. Again, Mother Teresa's political know-how came into use. As she traveled around the world, she met Catholics throughout the United States and Europe. She told them of her work in India and of her hopes and dreams for the future. Her ideas inspired many of her listeners, and they quickly recognized that Mother Teresa was a woman of her word. If she said that she wanted to create a successful group of international missions, then she would do it. They also recognized that they could provide the capital to help her make this possible. Many people began donating to the Missionaries of Charity, producing the funds necessary for the next stage in Mother Teresa's service to God. Indeed, the publicity and connections that she was able to generate during this trip would, in many ways, be just as important as her audience with the pope had been.

Chapter Ten: The Sisters of Charity Go International

During her audience with Pope John XXIII, Mother Teresa had asked him for the *decretum laudis*, or decree of praise. Receiving the decree of praise is extremely significant for a religious community such as the Missionaries of Charity. The decree of praise recognizes the success and maturity of a congregation and makes it subject no longer to a diocese but to the Holy See itself. It was this type of recognition that would grant Mother Teresa permission to expand the Sisters of Charity beyond India to become an international mission. Five years later, in 1965, Pope Paul VI granted her this decree.

Mother Teresa wasted little time. She decided to follow the same pattern of growth that had already proven so successful in India. The sisters would go to a new location and open up a house from which to serve the poorest and most destitute of the land—those who, like the untouchables of India, had been brushed aside and forgotten by their fellow citizens and neighbors. Once the house had been established, the sisters would begin to develop schools, orphanages, homes for the dying, and leper colonies, if applicable. Continuing to follow the lessons she had learned from the dinners her mother hosted so many years earlier, Mother Teresa would make the most of the money she had at hand. While ensuring that the mission provided adequate care to those who came there for help, they would always find ways to stretch their pennies so that they were able to serve all who were in need of their love and attention. They would also continue to wear the blue and white sari, as Mother Teresa had first donned years earlier, making them instantaneously recognizable throughout the world.

When determining where she would open her first house, Mother Teresa turned to an Australian archbishop and future cardinal named James Knox. Knox had been serving in India for 10 years and had seen first-hand the impressive work and successes that Mother Teresa's tenacity had made possible. He had become one of her strongest supporters and advocates. Therefore, when he heard of the growing need in Venezuela, he recommended Mother Teresa as the perfect person to take up the challenge. In July of 1965, Mother Teresa and the Sisters of Charity opened up their first mission outside of India, a home in Cocorote, Venezuela.

The Venezuelan venture was wildly successful, and it affirmed Mother Teresa's plan to follow the pattern laid out in India. Building on their success, the Sisters quickly expanded. In 1967, they opened a home in Sri Lanka. This was followed, in 1968, by homes in Tanzania, Austria, and the slums of Rome.

In 1971, she even fulfilled the dream ignited by her trip to America a decade earlier and opened up a home in New York City. In every case, the Sisters of Charity went to parts of the world that had populations in need and who were not being served by their fellow citizens and neighbors; in short, they went where they were most needed and could do the most good.

In 1969, she was awarded the Jawaharlal Nehru Award for International Understanding. The Indian government awards the prize yearly to one individual, of any nationality, whom they find has made an "outstanding contribution to the promotion of international understanding, goodwill and friendship among people of the world." True, it was only the first of many awards to come for Mother Teresa; however, this award, given at the time that it was, is perhaps particularly symbolic. For one thing, it seems quite fitting that she be recognized by her adopted country. The award recognized the work that she had been doing not only in India but also throughout the world. In this way, the award serves as a tangible marker of the monumental transition taking place in her life. It is almost as if, by awarding her an international award, India was recognizing that she was no longer theirs alone; they realized that, now and in the future, they would be sharing her with all peoples and nations.

This award also serves as a testament to Mother Teresa's ever-evolving understanding of who "her people" were. She had begun life with a quite narrow definition, recognizing her connection only with other Catholic Albanians. Under the influence of her mother, she had challenged this understanding as a young girl and started to see her connection with those of other ethnicities and religions who lived around her. She had then moved to India, recognizing her connection not only to those of her home region but also to those of her newly adopted land. Yet again, she began to challenge this understanding by moving into the slums and living with those individuals deemed untouchable by traditional Indian society. Now no one could deny that even the least of the least were her people and her neighbors. She had gone to the people who most needed her and given herself to them, and in turn they saw and accepted her as one of their own. She further solidified this transformation by expanding her missions internationally. It was not only the poorest of the poor in India with whom she identified herself but the poorest of the world as well, wherever they might be.

The step to take the Sisters of Charity international ensured the lasting success of the revolutionary changes that Mother Teresa was making to missionary work during the 20th century. She showed the world that all people everywhere, no matter how sick or destitute, no matter how forgotten or ignored by their fellow citizens and neighbors, were God's children and that, for this reason, they were her people as well. Mother Teresa had seen first-hand a number of turbulent events that pointed to the radical ways in which the world was changing. First, in her homeland, she saw the increasingly violent tensions between ethnic groups and the faltering of European stability. Then, in India, she witnessed the violent effects of decolonization. Mother Teresa, ever politically aware, knew that the world was fundamentally shifting and, if missionary work was going to continue to do God's will and serve the living Christ, then it would have to transform, too. More specifically, missionary practices that had developed during, and found support in, colonial expansion would have to be radically rethought. Missionaries could no longer maintain a separation from those they served, for this was increasingly seen as maintaining outdated colonial habits and, furthermore, often overlooked those who had been excluded from those systems and left most in need. Now, thanks to Mother Teresa, missionaries would go to the people and become one with them. Mother Teresa's rapid international growth pointed overwhelmingly to the success of this new approach.

Chapter Eleven: The Muggeridge Interview, Film, and Book

While Mother Teresa's first international trip in 1960 revealed her growing celebrity amongst the world's Catholics, one event in particular is credited with skyrocketing her to fame throughout the whole of the Western world. In 1968, she agreed to do an interview for the BBC with a then-renowned reporter named Malcolm Muggeridge. Immediately, a number of her closest aides and supports were against the idea, begging her to rescind the offer. Muggeridge had made a name for himself by loudly and publicly stating his own atheistic beliefs as well as his opposition to all forms of religion. He was also known for being an abrasive interviewer who enjoyed taking oppositional and negative positions in his work. Mother Teresa's supporters feared that he would conduct an unfair interview and would attempt to discredit the "little woman from India" and attempt to make a mockery of her.

Mother Teresa, however, was unmoved by such concerns and calmly asserted that she would go on with the interview. Here was a woman who had put her full faith in God. She knew that she had been called by Jesus to do the work she was doing; what care did she have for the way in which other might attempt to present it? It was a risk, nonetheless, but a risk worth taking. Never losing sight of the political and organizational needs of her (now international) religious community, this interview, if successful, would be exactly the type of publicity that the Sisters of Charity needed. The more the world heard of their good deeds, the more missions and services they would be able to open and maintain.

Thus, Muggeridge and Mother Teresa met in London to conduct the interview. To the surprise of all involved—well, all save Mother Teresa, perhaps—the two got along splendidly, and the interview was a great success. The BBC replayed it multiple times to an ever-growing audience. Mother Teresa, of course, had made it her life's work to show the world that all people were her people; she had connected with the poor around the world, so why not add a brash British atheist to the list as well? Muggeridge had apparently gone into the interview expecting Mother Teresa to be proud, overbearing, and judgmental. Instead, he found himself in conversation with a woman who spoke in simple and unassuming terms about the incredible work that she was doing. Her primary and overwhelming concern was always the love she felt for the poorest of the poor and her drive to help them in any way she could. She had little time to worry about people such as Muggeridge and even less time to judge them. God's people were her people, and this included Muggeridge, whatever his views might be.

Muggeridge was greatly moved by Mother Teresa's simple yet profound message of love. He found himself thinking repeatedly about the things she had said to him during their interview. As a result, Muggeridge entered into a crisis of faith, if one can apply such a term to a dedicated atheist. He even began to explore the Christianity that he had condemned for so long. In 1969, he began practicing the faith and wrote a book about his experience, entitled *Jesus Rediscovered.*

The interview had not only affected Muggeridge but had impacted his BBC viewers as well. Funds began pouring in to the Sisters of Charity, despite the fact that Mother Teresa never asked for money during the interview. Instead, people simply understood the great work that she was doing and wanted to find some way to support her. Clearly, Mother Teresa's new approach to missionary work was speaking to people. As the Sisters continued to grow internationally, this type of publicity and support would become an increasingly important component of their work.

In the same year as his conversion, Muggeridge decided to visit Mother Teresa in India. His plan was to make a documentary film about her work. Incredibly, they shot the film in only five days and did not encounter any of the typical equipment failures or other obstacles that so often plague on-location shootings in an exotic place. If this were not miracle enough, Muggeridge himself claims to have encountered a miracle when they were shooting at one of the Sisters' many homes for the dying. According to Muggeridge, his cameraman did not think it would be possible to shoot in the dark space. Muggeridge, however, thought that it was essential to introduce the world to all of Mother Teresa's work, perhaps most especially the way she cared for those so close to death without fear or judgment. Then, almost as if on cue, according to Muggeridge's account, the room was filled with a warm and bright light, making it possible for them to film inside the building.

The film was called *Something Beautiful for God* and met with almost instantaneous international support. Muggeridge followed up the film two year later with a book about Mother Teresa, also called *Something Beautiful for God*, which has now been translated into at least 13 languages. The title of the film comes from a letter that Mother Teresa wrote to Muggeridge shortly after his visit to India. In it she tells Muggeridge that he should, in his own way, "try to make the world conscious that it is never too late to do something beautiful for God."

According to many, it was the film and book that launched Mother Teresa into international fame. With these two pieces, people around the world, whether Catholic or not, were introduced to the daunting work to which she had committed her life.

Let us pause to consider the words of Mother Teresa that became the inspiration for this film and movie. They were, of course, meant for Muggeridge and most likely were addressing his late-in-life turn toward Christianity. However, they could have been referring just as readily to Mother Teresa's own life. As we have seen, Mother Teresa was never satisfied with her work; she was always searching for ways in which she might continue to serve God. It was this drive that compelled her to leave Saint Mary's after almost 20 years as a successful teacher and principal, and it was the same drive that led her to look beyond the borders of India and to concern herself with the world's poor. Not only was it never too late to do something beautiful for God but it was also never too late to do something *more* beautiful for God. In this quote, we find Mother Teresa teaching us always to be on the lookout for new ways to serve God, whether by actions we had not previously considered or by serving poor and destitute individuals of whom we had not previously been aware. In these words, Mother Teresa challenges us always to remain open and to be prepared to encounter God, perhaps often where we least expect to find Him.

The film brought the Sisters of Charity international fame, and it served an important role in the new missionary framework that Mother Teresa had developed. One of the most notable changes Mother Teresa had introduced to missionary work in the 20th century was her directive to go to the people one was serving and become one with them. For Mother Teresa, as she had seen so many times in her life, it was essential that individuals tear down the ethnic, religious, and social borders that divided them from one another. In some ways, the film and book were a means of doing just that. For many in the West, it was easy to remain unaware of poverty in the world, such as the situation of untouchables in India. These were people whom Westerners did not encounter on a daily basis. In fact, given the way in which many Western cities developed, many Westerners did not even interact with the poor and destitute in their own communities. This film, then, served as a wake-up call for many. Not only did it introduce Westerners to the plight of people in India but it also offered them a role model. Mother Teresa was only a little woman in a simple blue and white sari who had devoted her life to loving these individuals and improving their lives. If she could do such a thing, then others too could begin to address the poverty and suffering of their neighbors. Moreover, the film and book prompted many Westerners to think about how they defined "their people," in the same way that Mother Teresa was always looking to expand the definition of who "her people" were: Whom were they going to love, and to whom were they going to commit themselves to helping in the hour of need?

While a huge number of Westerners took up this call by offering financial support to the Sisters of Charity and their many projects around the world, some went even further. In 1970, the Sisters of Charity received 139 new candidates. Unlike in previous years, this year's group of candidates consisted of individuals from all over the world. These were individuals who had learned of Mother Teresa's good work and had heeded her call that, to serve God, one must love those most in need and become one with them through service, no matter who they are or where they might be.

By 1975, thanks to the incredible increase in donations initiated by Mother Teresa's ever-growing prominence and popularity, the Sisters of Charity had been able to open 32 homes for the dying, 67 colonies for lepers, and 28 children's homes in locations around the world. What could Mother Teresa hope to achieve next?

Chapter Twelve: The Nobel Peace Prize and Other Awards

What followed for Mother Teresa, besides the continuing development of the Sisters' of Charity work around the world, was a number of significant awards.

In 1971, she was awarded the first Pope John XXIII Peace Prize by Pope Paul VI. The award was not to be given annually; rather it was developed to be given only to an exceptional individual who was doing exceptional work to promote peace in the world. By selecting Mother Teresa as its first recipient, Paul VI was setting the bar high. Indeed, the award has only been given out a handful of times since. This must have been an especially significant award for Mother Teresa, as the religion to which she had devoted her life returned her devotion by acknowledging the importance of her life's innovative work. Furthermore, her labors were revolutionizing the way in which Catholic missionaries approached the world and the way in which the world perceived this work. Mother Teresa was an incredibly positive influence in the world for Catholicism, and the Church recognized this and made its appreciation known.

In 1979, at the age of 69, she was awarded the Nobel Peace Prize. In fact, this was not the first year she had been nominated; she had been nominated but passed over for the award three previous times. One of the strongest advocates for her nomination and selection for the award was Robert McNamara, who was a former American Defense secretary and the director of the World Bank at the time. In Mother Teresa's work, he found levels of success in serving the poor that were unthinkable in the organization where he worked, and he greatly admired her for this. He had worked for a number of years to have her awarded the Nobel.

Upon learning of her selection for the award, Mother Teresa told reporters in India, "I accept the prize in the name of the poor ... The prize is the recognition of the poor world ... By serving the poor I am serving Him." She went to Oslo to accept the prize. She asked that the extravagant banquet traditionally held in honor of the recipient be canceled and requested that all expenses be donated to the poor. She did decide to give a speech in front of the Hague, as was customary. As she had many years ago in Las Vegas in front of the National Council for Catholic Women, and again in her interview with Muggeridge, she spoke simply and from the heart. Speaking of love, that seemingly simple yet profound commandment, she explained: "It is not enough for us to say: I love God, but I do not love my neighbor. St. John says you are a liar if you say you love God and you don't love your neighbor. How can you love God whom you do not see, if you do not love your neighbor whom you see, whom you touch, with whom you live? ... We have been created in his image. We have been created to love and be loved, and then he has become man to make it possible for us to love as he loved us. He makes himself the hungry one—the naked one—the homeless one—the sick one—the one in prison—the lonely one—the unwanted one—and he says: You did it to me." In this quotation, Mother Teresa reveals to us the constant struggle that we must face if we are to love as Jesus commands us. For it is in those very moments when we least feel like loving someone—when we want to turn away from, blame, or ignore him or her—that she challenges us to see God in this individual and to love that person. Every time we find ourselves confronting another who is different from us in some way, whether by location, religion, ethnicity, or social status, we must work to see beyond and tear down those divisions, recognizing that other people are our neighbors— that we are all one and we are all God's people.

In 1980, she was awarded the Bharat Ratna, or Jewel of India, award. It is the highest honor that can be bestowed on an Indian civilian, and Mother Teresa is the only naturalized citizen to have ever won. Much like the Jawaharlal Nehru

Award awarded her in 1969, this particular award must have had special significance for Mother Teresa. However, whereas the Jawaharlal Nehru recognized her work both in India and abroad, the Jewel of India went one step further and acknowledged that this work was done by an Indian citizen worthy of honor. It must have seemed like ages, maybe even lifetimes, ago that she had left the Sisters of Loreto and decided to become an Indian citizen. Now, all of these years later, the country of which she had dreamed, and which she had accepted as her own, reciprocated this love, recognizing her as not merely one of their own but also as one of their most upstanding citizens.

In 1985, Mother Teresa was given the honor of addressing the United Nations General Assembly
on the occasion of its 40th anniversary. When introducing her, Secretary General Pérez de Cuélliar said what many around the world felt: "I don't think I need to present her. She doesn't need words. She does need deeds. I think that the best thing I can do is to pay tribute to her and to tell that she is much more than I, much more than all of us. She is the United Nations. She is peace in this world."

It was not only the West that recognized the significant impact Mother Teresa was making on the world. In 1987, the USSR honored her by bestowing upon her the Gold Medal of the Soviet Peace Committee. Obviously, in 1987, an individual would have to be quite exceptional for both the West and the USSR to honor him or her. But of course, it is perhaps not surprising that Mother Teresa was such as person.

Chapter Thirteen: Mother Teresa and the Crisis in Beirut

In 1982, war broke out between Israel and Lebanon. The years leading up to the war had been a tumultuous time for the Middle East. Lebanon in particular had felt the effects of these times as it had been entrenched in an overt civil war since 1975. The war erupted, at least in part, because of the unleashing of ethnic and religious tensions as the Middle East went through its own process of decolonization. In Lebanon alone, there was fighting between Sunni and Shiite Muslim factions, Christians, as well as ethnic Palestinians. The Palestinian Liberation Organization had become increasingly organized and militarized. This, in turn, raised the suspicions of Israel, Lebanon's neighbor to the south. With its own sizable minority population of Palestinians, Israel was heavily invested in and concerned by the PLO's activities and, thus, the fighting in Lebanon in general.

The tensions between Israel and Lebanon came to a head on June 3, 1982, when the Israeli Ambassador Shlomo Argov was shot and seriously wounded in London. The attack was attributed to the Abu Nidal terrorist organization, the headquarters of which were in Lebanon. The Israelis used the attack as justification for launching an offensive into southern Lebanon, where the Palestinian Liberation Organization was taking refuge. Only seven days later, the Israelis had surrounded Beirut, Lebanon's capital city. For the next seven weeks, they attacked the city by air, ground, and sea in what has become known as the Siege of Beirut. With intentions of ending the fighting quickly and decisively, the Israeli offensive was intense and brutal in order to overwhelm Beirut swiftly.

Into the middle of all of this chaos and violence stepped Mother Teresa. She had been asked by Pope John Paul II to act as his personal emissary during the conflict. The Pope's selection of Mother Teresa for this role was strategic for a number of reasons. Firstly, she was by this time recognized worldwide as a symbol of peace. If the Catholic Church wanted to express its hope that the violence be stopped and the conflict ended, who better to bring this message than Mother Teresa? Furthermore, Mother Teresa was loved and respected around the world, not only by Catholics but also by people of all races, creeds, and walks of life. For this reason, her presence ensured neutrality on the part of the Catholic Church.

However, we ought not discount the importance of Mother Teresa's historical background and political acumen. Although the actors and tensions were different than those in the Balkans, Mother Teresa was intimately aware of the way in which religious and ethnic opposition can rip a region apart. She also had experience, beginning with those dinners her mother had hosted so long ago, of dissolving these differences in order to unite people. Finally, Mother Teresa was the leader of an overwhelmingly successful international religious order. She clearly understood how to deal with the inevitable politics that would arise in such a situation, and she would be able to transfer this knowledge to her activities in the Middle East.

She arrived in Lebanon on August 11th, a month into the siege. She was closely followed by a huge throng of media. Everyone wanted to know what the "little lady from India" could do in the face of something as seemingly intractable as Middle Eastern politics. The media's attention made it difficult for her to do much covertly, but two days later she was nevertheless able to slip past the crowds and sneak into a part of Beirut that was seeing the worst of the fighting. She was going to visit what she thought was an Islamic home for the dying that many believed had been hit by Israeli artillery. However, when she reached the hospital, what she found was not the sick and elderly but, rather, 37 scared and injured children, refugees who had been left behind and were trapped in the hospital.

Mother Teresa quickly decided that she had to save these children; however, the fighting was so intense that no one knew how she would be able to accomplish this goal without getting herself killed. But of course, the "little lady from India" was not to be underestimated, including in her political tenacity. Speaking with both sides in the conflict, Mother Teresa was able to broker a momentary cease-fire that provided her and the children with safe passage to a Red Cross camp, which was located away from the fighting. Mother Teresa took the children there, where her Sisters could go about caring for them.

Can we imagine any other individual in the world capable of accomplishing such a feat? Rare is the person who is able to bring two warring factions to the table in order to broker a peace deal; even rarer is the individual who is able to do so in the Middle East. Mother Teresa truly was a phenomenal individual touched by God.

This incident was also exemplary of the extent to which Mother Teresa believed that love could reach. As she had said at the UN, it was not enough to love God abstractly; one must show this love by caring for one's neighbor. And who were Mother Teresa's neighbors? As we have seen, her understanding of who "her people" were had continually evolved. However, by 1982, as an international figure and Nobel Prize Winner, it was clear that the whole world was Mother Teresa's neighbor. If individuals were in danger or pain, Mother Teresa too felt this pain and was compelled to do something to ameliorate it, even if that meant risking her own life by walking into an active war zone and standing up to world powers. Indeed, Mother Teresa's love knew no bounds.

Mother Teresa was 72 years old at the time of the Lebanon War; however, despite her age, this conflict marked the transition into yet another phase of her life. Before the conflict, Mother Teresa's international actions had revolved primarily around opening missions and securing support and backing for those missions. Now, however, as the Beirut Crisis had shown, Mother Teresa was discovering that her presence alone could be a significant step in resolving conflicts and addressing the plight of the poorest of the poor around the world. In the years to come, Mother Teresa would use this ability—the ability to insert herself into situations—in order to create peace, time and time again.

Chapter Fourteen: Mother Teresa's Involvement in Other Global Crises

There are three world events of particular note during this period of Mother Teresa's life: the disaster in Bhopal, the Ethiopian famine, and the nuclear leak at Chernobyl. In every case, Mother Teresa inserted herself into the situation, using her physical presence to bring international attention to the devastation and thereby bring peace and aid to the suffering.

On the evening of December 2, 1984, in Bhopal, India, there was a horrible chemical gas leak at a pesticide factory owned by Union Carbide India Limited. The disaster spewed poisonous gases into the air, which were then carried by the winds throughout the region. Estimates suggest that over 500,000 people were affected by the leak. The immediate death toll that night was 2,259. Other estimates suggest that, within weeks, as many as 16,000 people had died from complications caused by exposure to the gas. Many more were maimed months and years later by diseases brought on by the chemicals. The region was left contaminated, and its population was devastated. To make things worse, neither the company nor the Indian government acted swiftly to contain the leak or to set up services for the victims. The suffering was massive. However, the West had heard little of the events in Bhopal, and thus no entities outside of the government or company were stepping in to help the victims, either.

Mother Teresa changed all of this. Hearing of the suffering in Bhopal, she quickly decided to go on a visit to the region, in order to bring comfort to the maimed and dying. Given her international celebrity, the world was of course interested to see what the purpose of Mother Teresa's latest trip was. This was when the situation in Bhopal was revealed to many. Shortly after her trip, funding and aide began to pour into the region.

The following year, in 1985, a devastating famine was in full swing in Ethiopia. It was brought on for a variety of reasons, including decolonization followed by years of wars; a massive, extended drought; and government corruption that wasted money on military concerns rather than feeding its citizens. The world, however, paid little heed to the situation in the region, even as the death toll skyrocketed. Indeed, the UN puts the number of deaths caused by the famine as high as one million. Again, upon hearing of the situation in the region, Mother Teresa decided to travel there in order to visit with and comfort the people, and again the word took notice of her activities. Her presence in Ethiopia was both a reality check and a challenge. It was a reality check insofar as it forced many in the West to consider events in a region of the world whose people were all too often ignored by larger global powers. It was a challenge insofar as Mother Teresa's presence demanded that the world see the people of Ethiopia as their neighbors, recognizing in their suffering the suffering of Christ.

Then, on April 26, 1986, near Pripyat, Ukraine, there were complications in reactor number four of the Chernobyl Nuclear Power Plant. The situation quickly escalated, and a huge fire broke out throughout the plant. The fire, in turn, emitted a massive plume of radioactive material that affected areas of the globe stretching from Europe to Russia. Thirty-one people died in the immediate aftermath of the event, many of them emergency personnel working to contain the fallout. However, the numbers of those who have developed cancer and other health issues attributable to radiation poisoning is expected to reach into the thousands as time goes on. Furthermore, there has been a spike in the number of birth defects in regions most impacted by the fallout. With the Cold War still in full swing at the time of the disaster, the Iron Curtain separating the USSR from the West meant that the West was unable to obtain much information about the disaster. They had no idea exactly how devastating the event had been and how far the contamination stretched. Mother

Teresa decided to travel to the region upon hearing about the event. The role her presence played in this event is a bit different from that in the two other events just discussed, for in this instance her presence did not simply bring to light an event about which much of the world knew nothing. Her presence, rather, also opened up communications between two world superpowers amidst a decades-long standoff.

If one were simply to look at Mother Teresa's travels in the 1980s with little regard for her history and political sensibilities, one might be surprised at her seemingly uncanny ability to show up in extremely significant places during extremely significant events. However, we know that the story is much more complicated than this. While Mother Teresa's travels certainly were compelled by God and her desire to love her neighbor to the fullest extent possible, including by traveling to areas afflicted by war, natural disaster, or chemical threat, we might also see another side to them as well. One might argue that Mother Teresa had never really lost the political tenacity on which her father had taught her to rely. This was obvious throughout Mother Teresa's life, beginning with the way in which she was able to navigate the Indian government in order to find funding for her first schools.

However, these three events and her other travels during this time period perhaps most starkly point toward the depths of her political talent. Unlike her father, she never used her political sensibilities to create oppositions or to capitalize upon them. Rather, she astutely used her presence to intervene in highly polarized situations in order to offer the neutral and universal message of love of neighbor. In every case, Mother Teresa must have been aware that she was putting herself at risk by traveling to these dangerous locations; however, she calculated that this risk was worth it if it would shed light on a situation and challenge the world to re-imagine who their neighbor was so that they might love others all the more. If she could force the world's hand by intervening in these situations through her mere presence, then how could she value her own life more highly? How better could she serve God?

Chapter Fifteen: Mother Teresa and the AIDS Crisis—the "New Leprosy" of the West

There is one other significant crisis of the 1980s with which Mother Teresa became involved and of which it is important to take note. It again exemplifies the extent to which Mother Teresa asked us to love our neighbors. In addition, however, it demonstrates the way in which Mother Teresa was always open to the changing world around her. As new crises and forms of suffering emerged, she was always ready to confront them with an open mind in order to determine how best to serve the people who most needed her help.

New York City had bothered Mother Teresa since she had visited it on her first international trip so long ago. She simply could not fathom how the richest and most powerful nation in the world could also have the slums and destitution that existed in New York. This was perhaps especially the case with New York in the 1980s. How was it possible that those more fortunate were not helping their neighbors, their fellow citizens, in their hour of need?

When the AIDS crisis came to New York City in the 1980s, it decimated certain populations, especially homosexual men and illicit drug users. On first thought, it might seem strange to think that Mother Teresa felt compelled to take up of the cause of these individuals. However, on second thought, it is perfectly understandable, for both of these populations were pushed to the edges of society. They were often ignored and, thus, had to suffer alone without recourse to aid or resources. In so many ways, they were like the untouchables of India, with whom she had first begun to work so long ago.

In fact, Mother Teresa made this connection publicly when she announced that she believed AIDS was quickly becoming the "new leprosy" of the West. The connection is, indeed, uncanny. Like lepers, people un-afflicted by the disease were often scared to interact with the victims in any way. People refused to hug and kiss suffering family members, and many people were left to die alone in isolated hospital rooms.

The initial response to the AIDS crisis, as is well known, was to blame the individuals who had become infected by it and to judge them for their "risky" behavior. Mother Teresa was unmotivated by such arguments. Who was she to judge a person in pain? Who was she to judge another's suffering? For her, love was greater than any of these arguments. She knew that no matter what these individuals had done, they were still God's children, they were still her neighbors, and she loved them; and to love them meant to join with them in order to determine how she might serve them.

She opened up a hospice in Greenwich Village, where her sisters cared for individuals who were suffering from the disease and had nowhere else to turn. Her compassion for those afflicted with AIDS and her refusal to judge them for their actions even led her to call for and gain the release of three young men from Sing Sing Prison. All three men were suffering from advanced cases of the illness, and Mother Teresa was adamant that even they, these men who had chosen to break the laws of the land, should not have to die alone, locked away in a cell. Even they deserved to be loved and cared for in their hour of need. She had them transferred to the hospice, where her sisters cared for them until their deaths.

But what exactly is noteworthy in Mother Teresa's response to the AIDS crisis in America? Surely it was not the first disease she had decided to combat, nor was it somehow more significant than the other issues upon which she chose to focus. However, unlike other diseases, AIDS was a newly emerging disease in the early 1980s and one about which the world knew little at the time. It carried with it a social stigma perhaps not even found with leprosy, which was stigmatized but also, at least, understood by many. None of this influenced

Mother Teresa; she refused to judge anyone, for any reason, no matter how contemporary or popular such prejudices might be. Again, we find the extent to which Mother Teresa was willing to love others and what it meant for her to love Jesus and to love her neighbor. It also demonstrates the way in which she constantly challenged herself to push the limits of this love. In a moment when it would have been so easy to follow social convention and look the other way and find a different disease to address, she instead challenged herself to find Christ in the pain and suffering of these individuals and to seek out how she might serve them.

Mother Teresa's response to the AIDS crisis in America also serves as yet another example of the way in which the political sensibilities she learned from her father helped her to carry out her mission to its fullest. Unlike her father, she did not use her skills and knowledge to draw divisions between individuals. Instead, as this particular example indicates, she used her knowledge to anticipate the development of such divisions. In calling AIDS the "new leprosy" of the West, she was attempting to warn the world. She was attempting to show people that, yet again, they were threatening to turn a blind eye to their fellow man and to the newest embodiment of the suffering Christ, who most needed their love and affection.

Mother Teresa was a woman ahead of her time. She was always aware of the changing social situation, whether that be the political system in India as it transitioned from colonial rule to democracy or the response to AIDS in the 1980s, and she used her political awareness to act upon these developments. This is yet another change that Mother Teresa introduced to missionary work in the 20th century. Missionaries could no longer assume that they knew who most needed their services. Rather, in a world of political and social upheaval, one had to constantly remain vigilant and open-minded as world events continuously produced new and often unanticipated victims.

Chapter Sixteen: The Teachings of Mother Teresa and the Sisters of Charity

In 1976, the contemplative branch of the Sisters of Charity was established. But what were the teachings of this particular religious community? Like many other orders of nuns, the Sisters of Charity took vows of chastity, poverty, and obedience. Their possessions were kept to a minimum. No matter where they served in the world, they were issued only three of the blue and white saris, with the intention that they would then have one to wear, one to wash, and one to mend. They were given only two or three cotton habits as well as a girdle and pair of sandals. Of course, they also always carried a crucifix and rosary with them, as well as a prayer book, and they kept all of their belongings in a simple canvas bag. If they happened to live in a part of the world with a colder climate, they were also allowed to have a sweater and even a coat, scarf, and warm shoes. However, all of these items were only kept out of necessity.

The Sisters of Charity also adhered to a fourth vow: to give "wholehearted free service to the poorest of the poor." Mother Teresa's life, of course, serves as the ultimate example of this vow. Her teachings and speeches also help us to understand that "wholehearted" service to the poor means constantly challenging oneself to see one's neighbor in the poor and afflicted around us. This is especially important when one feels an aversion to such thinking. Whether this aversion arises from ignorance—one is simply unaware of the suffering around oneself and throughout the world—or from social and political stigma, it does not matter. Mother Teresa and the Sisters of Charity worked vigilantly to overcoming such divisions, making this challenge their life's labor. It was only by undergoing this strenuous and self-reflective work that, Mother Teresa believed, one could truly enact love in the world, understand what it meant to love God, and love one's neighbor as oneself.

Although there were many different parts to the Missionaries of Charity, Mother Teresa used the image of the five wounds of Jesus to describe their connection to one another. The two wounds in Jesus' hands represented the sisters and brothers of the Missionaries of Charity who took action throughout the world and carried out God's will. The two wounds in Jesus' feet represented the contemplative sisters and brothers. These individuals went in search of their souls and served as the spiritual counterparts to their active brothers and sisters. The wound in Jesus' heart represented the priests who served the Missionaries of Charity, supporting and nurturing their work. The body of Christ itself represented the world's poor, in desperate need of the love and care that the Missionaries of

Charity were able to provide. It was love of this sacrificed body, the recognition of the suffering Christ in the suffering of those in the world, that united the world and made people one with each other.

The teachings of Mother Teresa can also be found in two of her favorite prayers. The first was written by Pope Paul VI:

Make us worthy, Lord,
to serve our fellow men
throughout the world who live and die
in poverty and hunger.
Give them through our hands,
this day their daily bread,
and by our understanding love,
give peace and joy.
Amen.

By repeating just these few phrases to himself or herself, an individual is able to recall the most significant aspects of the work done by the Missionaries of Charity. They saw the whole world as their neighbors and their fellow men, and they traveled around the world to serve them. Through their work, they aimed to bring relief to the afflicted and peace to the world.

The second prayer is a prayer by Saint Francis of Assisi, and it speaks not only to the actions of the Missionaries of Charity (as the previous prayer does) but also to the challenge that ought to guide these actions. It reads:

Lord, make me a channel of your peace, that
  where there is hatred, I may bring love;
  where there is wrong, I may bring the spirit of
    forgiveness;
  where there is discord, I may bring harmony;
  where there is error, I may bring truth;
  where there is doubt, I may bring faith;
  where there is despair, I may bring hope;
  where there are shadows, I may bring light;
  where there is sadness, I may bring joy.
Lord, grant that I may seek rather
  to comfort than to be comforted;
  to understand than to be understood;
  to love than to be loved;
  for it is by forgetting self that one finds;
  it is by forgiving that one is forgiven;

it is by dying that one awakens to eternal life.

Amen.

In short, the teachings of the Missionaries of Charity were grounded in a development and modernization of that simple lesson Mother Teresa learned from her mother when she was only a little girl: love thy neighbor as thyself. However, Mother Teresa showed the world that, in the rapidly changing times of the 20th century, this simple phrase was more complex than it might at first seem. For the 20th century was a world that saw two world wars, ethnic and political strife the world over, the emergence of new diseases, and natural and human-made disasters on a scale unthinkable in previous time-periods. In such a world, one's "neighbor" was no longer a simple concept. Rather, one had to challenge oneself to remain open to the changing times, constantly aware that one's neighbors might be the individuals one least expected. This meant that the act of loving one's neighbor became more complex. In order to ensure this love, one had to tear down the boundaries between oneself and others. Mother Teresa did this throughout her life, but she first did so when she decided to leave the confines of the Sisters of Loreto and live in the slums of Calcutta. To love, a person had to become one with those different from him or her; they had to recognize that all men, no matter their deeds or afflictions, were God's children and part of "their people."

One also had to consider the way in which one went about this love. It was not enough merely to say that one loved God or that one loved those who were different. Rather, one had to demonstrate this love through actions. Love meant recognizing the pain of others and attempting to ameliorate it, and it meant challenging oneself to do so in situations where one might be least likely or most unwilling to do so. Perhaps the most important teaching with which Mother Teresa left us is never to take this principle—to love thy neighbor as thyself—lightly or for granted, but rather to find in it the struggle necessary to create peace in the world.

Chapter Seventeen: Mother Teresa's Legacy and Beatification

In 1989, Mother Teresa finally began to slow down as she suffered a severe heart attack and her health began to decline. In 1990, she informed the pope that she wanted to resign as the leader of the Missionaries of Charity. However, they quickly realized that there was no one who could take her place. It was not simply that no one else could serve as a figure of hope and beacon of peace in the way that Mother Teresa did. Indeed, it would have been unfair to expect such things from any other individual. However, they also could not find anyone with the political acumen and organizational intelligence necessary to carry out the job that Mother Teresa did. And so, as we have seen numerous times now throughout her life, she thought little of herself and her own deteriorating body and continued to work and serve her people.

By 1997, the work had finally become too much. On March 13, 1997, Mother Teresa stepped down as the leader of the Missionaries of Charity. She was succeeded by Sister Nirmala Joshi. Sister Nirmala's parents were from Nepal, and she had grown up in British India. She was raised Hindu but converted to Catholicism after being educated in Christian schools. She had a background in political science and legal studies and had also started the contemplative branch of the Missionaries of Charity. In Sister Nirmala, Mother Teresa finally found someone who could fill her shoes. Sister Nirmala had the political smarts necessary to run a worldwide organization, but she also had the religious background and conviction to ensure that this political work was always carried out in the name of love of God and the suffering Christ.

On September 5, 1997, Mother Teresa died from heart, lung, and kidney problems. She was 87 years old. She died in peace in Calcutta, India, her adopted homeland. The government of India issued a state funeral for her, and thousands of Indians—thousands of her people—lined the streets to say goodbye to the little lady who had brought peace to the world. She is buried at the Mother House of the Missionaries of Charity in Calcutta, the place where so many of her hopes and dreams first became realities. Today, many travel to this site to pay tribute to her and her work as well as to be inspired to continue that work themselves.

Mother Teresa was a woman who had lived multiple lives. In her first life, she had been a school-teacher and principal. In her next life, she had started and become the leader of a successful religious order. She then took on a number of new roles once this order went international, and she became a beacon of peace throughout the world. Finally, she became an emblem of peace herself, traveling around the world and using her presence to draw attention to disasters throughout the world and the victims they produced. And yet, Mother Teresa was only human. We ought not think that she did not face any struggles of her own throughout her life. This became most apparent when, in 2003, three of her private correspondences were published, including the journals she was first asked to keep by the archbishop of Calcutta and had done so throughout her life. In these journals, one finds the intimate musings of a woman who suffered a crisis of faith, indeed for practically the last 50 years of her life. Faced with so much death and destruction, she often questioned God's plan for the world and whether He had forsaken it.

But we ought not be disheartened by this revelation—indeed, not at all. In the midst of all of her tremendous successes, it is easy to overlook Mother Teresa's humanity; it is easy to say that she was only able to achieve what she did because she was, in some way, greater than other humans. However, as her journals reveal, this was not the case. She confronted the same fears and uncertainties as anyone else does, at least at some point in their life. The commandment to love God by loving the suffering Christ in the poor of the world was something with which she thought others would struggle. It was something with which she often found herself struggling. For this reason, Mother Teresa ought to inspire us. If she carried within her soul many of the same thoughts and doubts that we do—if she was challenged to love others in the same way we often find ourselves to be challenged—then we can come to realize that her achievements are not beyond our reach. We, too, can do great things in the world, just as Mother Teresa did.

Many individuals quickly began calling Mother Teresa a saint after her death. The road to sainthood, of course, is a long one; however, hearing the calls of his people and of God, Pope John Paul II did what he could to speed up this process. Typically, one must wait five years after an individual's death before the sainthood process can begin. John Paul II, however, waived this time period in 1999, only two years after her death. Her name moved quickly through the first two steps of the process, being granted first the title of "Servant of God" and then of "Venerable."

Then, on October 19, 2003, Pope John Paul II beatified her, the third step on the road toward sainthood. This step granted her the title "Blessed" and could only come about through the recognition of a miracle. This miracle had taken place a year earlier. A woman named Monica Besra, who herself was not a Christian, had been suffering from a huge abdominal tumor. The Sisters of Charity prayed over the woman, asking Mother Teresa to watch over and protect her. They also place a locket with a picture of Mother Teresa on her stomach at the site of the tumor. The next day, the woman woke up to find that her tumor had disappeared.

This is the most recent step in the process toward sainthood for Mother Teresa. There is one final step that requires the recognition of a second miracle. While this has not yet taken place, there is little doubt that one day it will and that Mother Teresa will officially become a modern-day saint of the Catholic Church.

Conclusion

Mother Teresa was only a diminutive woman with a wide smile and a wrinkled face, yet she achieved greatness. She revolutionized modern Catholic missionary work. She started and led an international religious organization that served people in numerous ways throughout the world. She even brought peace to the Middle East, if only for a day. In short, she showed the world that, by re-imagining the meaning of family, people, and love, an individual could bring about peace.

In many ways, Mother Teresa's story does not end. We are still waiting for her sainthood, but her continuing story is more than just this. She serves as a role model for individuals everywhere. Her life teaches us (as she taught Muggeridge many years ago) that it is never too late to make a difference in the world. What is more, one must never be satisfied with what one has achieved but always seek out new ways in which one can achieve more. One can never do too much good in the world; one can never help too many people. Her life also teaches us that, although this task may seem daunting, especially in today's world, the first step is easy. All one needs to do is to follow in Mother Teresa's footsteps and step beyond the walls that separate one from those in need around them.

Please enjoy the first two chapters of Pope Francis: Pastor of Mercy, written by Michael J. Ruszala, as available from Wyatt North Publishing.

Pope Francis: Pastor of Mercy
Chapter 1

There is something about Pope Francis that captivates and delights people, even people who hardly know anything about him. He was elected in only two days of the conclave, yet many who tried their hand at speculating on who the next pope might be barely included him on their lists. The evening of Wednesday, March 13, 2013, the traditional white smoke poured out from the chimney of the Sistine Chapel and spread throughout the world by way of television, Internet, radio, and social media, signaling the beginning of a new papacy.

As the light of day waned from the Eternal City, some 150,000 people gathered watching intently for any movement behind the curtained door to the loggia of St. Peter's. A little after 8:00 p.m., the doors swung open and Cardinal Tauran emerged to pronounce the traditional and joyous Latin formula to introduce the new Bishop of Rome: "Annuncio vobis gaudium magnum; habemus papam!" ("I announce to you a great joy: we have a pope!") He then announced the new Holy Father's identity: "Cardinalem Bergoglio..."

The name Bergoglio, stirred up confusion among most of the faithful who flooded the square that were even more clueless than the television announcers were, who scrambled to figure out who exactly the new pope was. Pausing briefly, Cardinal

Tauran continued by announcing the name of the new pope: "...qui sibi nomen imposuit Franciscum" ("who takes for himself the name Francis"). Whoever this man may be, his name choice resonated with all, and the crowd erupted with jubilant cheers. A few moments passed before the television announcers and their support teams informed their global audiences that the man who was about to walk onto the loggia dressed in white was Cardinal Jorge Mario Bergoglio, age 76, of Buenos Aires, Argentina.

To add to the bewilderment and kindling curiosity, when the new pope stepped out to the thunderous applause of the crowd in St. Peter's Square, he did not give the expected papal gesture of outstretched arms. Instead, he gave only a simple and modest wave. Also, before giving his first apostolic blessing, he bowed asking the faithful, from the least to the greatest, to silently pray for him. These acts were only the beginning of many more words and gestures, such as taking a seat on the bus with the cardinals, refusing a popemobile with bulletproof glass, and paying his own hotel bill after his election, that would raise eyebrows among some familiar with papal customs and delight the masses.

Is he making a pointed critique of previous pontificates? Is he simply posturing a persona to the world at large to make a point? The study of the life of Jorge Mario Bergoglio gives a clear answer, and the answer is no. This is simply who he is as a man and as a priest. The example of his thought-provoking gestures flows from his character, his life experiences, his religious vocation, and his spirituality. This book uncovers the life of the 266th Bishop of Rome, Jorge Mario Bergoglio, also known as Father Jorge, a name he preferred even while he was an archbishop and cardinal.

What exactly do people find so attractive about Pope Francis? Aldo Cagnoli, a layman who developed a friendship with the Pope when he was serving as a cardinal, shares the following: "The greatness of the man, in my humble opinion lies not in building walls or seeking refuge behind his wisdom and office, but rather in dealing with everyone judiciously, respectfully, and with humility, being willing to learn at any moment of life; that is what Father Bergoglio means to me" (as quoted in Ch. 12 of Pope Francis: Conversations with Jorge Bergoglio, previously published as El Jesuita [The Jesuit]).

At World Youth Day 2013, in Rio de Janeiro, Brazil, three million young people came out to celebrate their faith with

Pope Francis. Doug Barry, from EWTN's Life on the Rock, interviewed youth at the event on what features stood out to them about Pope Francis. The young people seemed most touched by his authenticity. One young woman from St. Louis said, "He really knows his audience. He doesn't just say things to say things... And he is really sincere and genuine in all that he does." A friend agreed: "He was looking out into the crowd and it felt like he was looking at each one of us...." A young man from Canada weighed in: "You can actually relate to [him]... for example, last night he was talking about the World Cup and athletes." A young woman added, "I feel he means what he says... he practices what he preaches... he states that he's there for the poor and he actually means it."

The Holy Spirit guided the College of Cardinals in its election of Pope Francis to meet the needs of the Church following the historic resignation of Pope Benedict XVI due to old age. Representing the growth and demographic shift in the Church throughout the world and especially in the Southern Hemisphere, Pope Francis is the first non-European pope in almost 1,300 years. He is also the first Jesuit pope. Pope Francis comes with a different background and set of experiences. Both as archbishop and as pope, his flock knows him for his humility, ascetic frugality in solidarity with the poor, and closeness. He was born in Buenos Aires to a family of Italian immigrants, earned a diploma in chemistry, and followed a priestly vocation in the Jesuit order after an experience of God's mercy while receiving the sacrament of Reconciliation. Even though he is known for his smile and humor, the world also recognizes Pope Francis as a stern figure that stands against the evils of the world and challenges powerful government officials, when necessary.

The Church he leads is one that has been burdened in the West by the aftermath of sex abuse scandals and increased secularism. It is also a Church that is experiencing shifting in numbers out of the West and is being challenged with religious persecution in the Middle East, Asia, and Africa. The Vatican that Pope Francis has inherited is plagued by cronyism and scandal. This Holy Father knows, however, that his job is not merely about numbers, politics, or even success. He steers clear of pessimism knowing that he is the head of Christ's Body on earth and works with Christ's grace. This is the man God has chosen in these times to lead his flock.

Chapter 2: Early Life in Argentina

Jorge Mario Bergoglio was born on December 17, 1936, in the Flores district of Buenos Aires. The district was a countryside locale outside the main city during the nineteenth century and many rich people in its early days called this place home. By the time Jorge was born, Flores was incorporated into the city of Buenos Aires and became a middle class neighborhood. Flores is also the home of the beautiful Romantic-styled Basilica of San José de Flores, built in 1831, with its dome over the altar, spire over the entrance, and columns at its facade. It was the Bergoglios' parish church and had much significance in Jorge's life.

Jorge's father's family had arrived in Argentina in 1929, immigrating from Piedimonte in northern Italy. They were not the only ones immigrating to the country. In the late nineteenth century, Argentina became industrialized and the government promoted immigration from Europe. During that time, the land prospered and Buenos Aires earned the moniker "Paris of the South." In the late nineteenth and early twentieth centuries waves of immigrants from Italy, Spain, and other European countries came off ships in the port of Buenos Aires. Three of Jorge's great uncles were the first in the family to immigrate to Argentina in 1922 searching for better employment opportunities after World War I. They established a paving company in Buenos Aires and built a four-story building for their company with the city's first elevator. Jorge's father and paternal grandparents followed the brothers in order to keep the family together and to escape Mussolini's fascist regime in Italy. Jorge's father and grandfather also helped with the business for a time. His father, Mario, who had been an accountant for a rail company in Italy, provided similar services for the family business (Cardinal Bergoglio recalls more on the story of his family's immigration and his early life in Ch. 1 of Conversations with Jorge Bergoglio).

Providentially, the Bergoglios were long delayed in liquidating their assets in Italy; this forced them to miss the ship they planned to sail on, the doomed Pricipessa Mafalda, which sank off the northern coast of Brazil before reaching Buenos Aires. The family took the Giulio Cesare instead and arrived safely in Argentina with Jorge's Grandma Rosa. Grandma Rosa wore a fur coat stuffed with the money the family brought with them from Italy. Economic hard times eventually hit Argentina in 1932 and the family's paving business went under, but the Bergoglio brothers began anew.

Jorge's father, Mario, met his mother Regina at Mass in 1934. Regina was born in Argentina, but her parents were also Italian immigrants. Mario and Regina married the following year after meeting. Jorge, the eldest of their five children, was born in 1936. Jorge fondly recalls his mother gathering the children around the radio on Sunday afternoons to listen to opera and explain the story. A true porteño, as the inhabitants of the port city of Buenos Aires are called, Jorge liked to play soccer, listen to Latin music, and dance the tango. Jorge's paternal grandparents lived around the corner from his home. He greatly admired his Grandma Rosa, and keeps her written prayer for her grandchildren with him until this day. Jorge recalls that while his grandparents kept their personal conversations in Piedmontese, Mario chose mostly to speak Spanish, preferring to look forward rather than back. Still, Jorge grew up speaking both Italian and Spanish.

Upon entering secondary school at the age of thirteen, his father insisted that Jorge begin work even though the family, in their modest lifestyle, was not particularly in need of extra income. Mario Bergoglio wanted to teach the boy the value of work and found several jobs for him during his adolescent years. Jorge worked in a hosiery factory for several years as a cleaner and at a desk. When he entered technical school to study food chemistry, Jorge found a job working in a laboratory. He worked under a woman who always challenged him to do his work thoroughly. He remembers her, though, with both fondness and sorrow. Years later, she was kidnapped and murdered along with members of her family because of her political views during the Dirty War, a conflict in the 1970's and 80's between the military dictatorship and guerrilla fighters in which thousands of Argentineans disappeared.

Initially unhappy with his father's decision to make him work, Jorge recalls later in his life that work was a valuable formative experience for him that taught him responsibility, realism, and how the world operated. He learned that a person's self worth often comes from their work, which led him to become committed later in life to promote a just culture of work rather than simply encouraging charity or entitlement. He believes that people need meaningful work in order to thrive. During his boyhood through his priestly ministry, he experienced the gulf in Argentina between the poor and the well off, which left the poor having few opportunities for gainful employment.

At the age of twenty-one, Jorge became dangerously ill. He was diagnosed with severe pneumonia and cysts. Part of his upper right lung was removed, and each day Jorge endured the pain and discomfort of saline fluid pumped through his chest to clear his system. Jorge remembers that the only person that was able to comfort him during this time was a religious sister who had catechized him from childhood, Sister Dolores. She exposed him to the true meaning of suffering with this simple statement: "You are imitating Christ." This stuck with him, and his sufferings during that time served as a crucible for his character, teaching him how to distinguish what is important in life from what is not. He was being prepared for what God was calling him to do in life, his vocation.

Made in the USA
San Bernardino, CA
14 November 2017